The Road to Happiness

Psalm One

Jay E. Adams

Institute for Nouthetic Studies, a ministry of Mid-America Baptist Theological Seminary, 2095 Appling Road, Memphis, TN 38016

mabts.edu / nouthetic.org / INSBookstore.com

The Road to Happiness by Jay E. Adams

Copyright © 2020 by the Institute for Nouthetic Studies.

ISBN: 978-1-949737-19-6 (Print)
ISBN: 978-1-949737-20-2 (eBook)

Editor: Donn R. Arms
Design: James Wendorf | www.FaithfulLifePublishers.com

Names: Adams, Jay E., 1929-
Title: *The Road to Happiness* / Jay E. Adams
Memphis: Institute for Nouthetic Studies, 2020
Identifiers: ISBN 978-1-949737-19-6 (paper)
Classification: LCC BS1430.2 | DDC 223.2

All rights reserved. No part of this publication may be reproduced, stored in a retrieval system, or transmitted in any form or by any means – electronic, mechanical, photocopy, recording, or any other – except for brief quotations in printed reviews, without prior permission of the publisher.

Published in the United States of America

TABLE OF CONTENTS

Introduction 1

1. Happinesses 7
2. It's God from Whom all Blessings Flow 11
3. Walk, Stand, Sit 16
4. Standing … then Sitting 23
5. Staying off the Wrong Road 28
6. Delighting in Scripture 32
7. Meditating in the Bible 36
8. Like a Tree 43
9. The Human and the Divine 49
10. The Wicked 56
11. Wind-driven Souls 61
12. The Judgment 65
13. The Two Roads 69

INTRODUCTION

Appropriately, Psalm 1 stands at the beginning of the Psalter. In its antithetical setting forth of two ways – the way of the righteous, and the way of the wicked – it introduces us to the theme that runs throughout the Psalms: antithesis. Always, there is God's way, and then all others. There is no compromise between them; there is no third way! As a result, it firmly opposes the relativism of our times. And, equally appropriate are the conclusions reached about each of these two ways: while one is the way of happiness, the other is the way of eternal misery. Hedonists, everywhere, have missed the way of true joy and peace while seeking these in drugs and everywhere else.

The words of this Psalm, because of its sharply defined categories, are precisely what men and women in our time need desperately to hear. In nearly every book, movie, television show, and teaching context, a continuum mentality underlies what is said. Everything is a shade of gray; nothing is black and white. All belong somewhere along a continuum where it is declared to be somewhat true and somewhat false, partly right and partly wrong. Nothing is good or bad; correct or in error; such polarization is strictly frowned upon.[1] Consequently, men and women, children in the home and in school, are confused. Lines drawn today are erased tomorrow; viewpoints have become mere fads to be changed with the advent of every new idea. Nothing is nailed down; all is in flux.

Morality, along with this fad surfing (as one writer called it), has suffered the same fate as everything else. If they ever consider the matter, people wonder whether there is established divine truth upon which to depend or whether what they are taught today will disappear with the next breeze that carries it away. In a time of shifting sands, people tend to do "that which is right in their own eyes." And, because they

---

[1] Inconsistently, polarization is considered the one truly bad thing! Relativists tolerate every belief except that which teaches intolerance of false beliefs. Almost uniquely, Christianity – which holds to the words of Jesus in John 14:6 – is strongly condemned.

know that there is no basis outside themselves for such a standard of morality, they carry a sense of guilt but do not know why, or what to do about it.

It is into such a milieu of thought and practice, where pragmatism and expediency carry the day that this Psalm thrusts its knife-sharp message. It is precisely what the world needs – whether or not it knows so. Christians, too, must be awakened from the slumber that engulfs so many of them. Likewise, they have been sorely affected by the climate of the times. To them, Psalm 1 should come both as a warning and an inspiration. There are few words so ringingly clear and explicit as those found in the Psalm. They are words that every Christian needs to ponder in a time of compromise and opposition to all they hold dear. The Psalmist's words can so heighten their sense of direction and awareness of what God has to say about how to think and act in our day that every believer ought to read them over and over again.

It is to encourage that very thing that I have written and sent forth this short volume. It is my hope that it will become a clarion call to many who are succumbing to the evil influences of the world around them. It is my prayer, that being awakened by God through this Psalm, they will throw off the lethargy, shed the cynicism, and disavow the compromise that now weakens them. To that end, I suggest that you once more center your mind and heart upon Psalm One:

O the happinesses of the man

> *who has not walked in the counsel of the wicked,*
>
> *And has not stood in the way of sinners*
>
> *And has not sat in the seat of scoffers.*

But his delight is in the law of Yahweh alone,

> *And in His law he meditates day and night.*

Now, he will be like a tree that is planted by irrigating canals

> *Which will give forth its fruit in its season.*
>
> *And its leaf will not wither,*
>
> *And everything that he does he will cause to prosper.*

Not so are the wicked!

> *But they are only like chaff that the wind drives away.*

Consequently, the wicked will not stand in the judgment

> *Nor sinners in the company of the righteous,*

Since Yahweh knows the way of the righteous

> *And that the way of the wicked will end in ruin.*

These words, understood, appreciated, and applied to life today, can make all the difference in a Christian's walk. In this book, we shall explore them in depth to discover how they may do so. Get ready for a great experience in analyzing your lifestyle in the light of the Word of the living God!

Chapter One
HAPPINESSES

The very first words of the very first Psalm deal with ***happiness***. They read, "O, the happinesses of …" Today, for many, happiness is the *sine qua non* of life; it is the one thing they seek and think that they cannot live without. In their mad rush to obtain happiness, men, women, and children throw all else overboard. But the sad fact is that true happiness eludes them. The ephemeral happiness they know today does not last overnight. Today's sports thrill is tomorrow's defeat; today's business success is followed by tomorrow's slump in the stock market. Last night's sexual conquest is today's regret. Succinctly, the book of Hebrews pegs it for us all when it speaks of "the short-lived pleasures of sin" (Hebrews 11:25).

Not that all one does to obtain happiness in and of itself is sin, but even legitimate activities sought as the ultimate end of life seem to be, as Hebrews says, "short-lived." Because it is based upon happenings, this happiness lasts no longer than the reverberations of the latest happening. The happiness seeker may well ask, "What is lasting happiness? Can it ever be found? And, if so, can it be obtained?"

The Psalmist says, "yes!" He opens his Psalm with the words, "O, the happinesses of the man who…" What interesting words! The spell check simply fails to recognize the word "happinesses." The plural is beyond its reach. These multiple happinesses, one uninterruptedly taking the place of the next, are unknown to modern man. The term, as translated, is even poor English. But it is not poor theology! It is the Psalmist's way of telling us that there is such a thing as lasting happiness. And, he goes on in his Psalm to tell us what it is, where it can be found, and how one may attain it! Plainly, then, the modern seeker after happiness need not be left high and dry; he need not throw up his hands in despair. Just over the horizon lies the end of his quest. But he must take the right road, or he will altogether miss it. It is about the road to happiness that the first Psalm is concerned.

Most translations of the Hebrew term for happiness use the English word "blessedness." But that word is elusive; it is difficult for modern man to comprehend. It is better, therefore, to translate it "happiness" and then explain that it means infinitely more than that word as it is commonly used. Let me put it this way: Blessedness is God's kind of happiness.[1] The ordinary kind, which is based on happenings, is quite distinct from this. God-given happiness is lasting, because it rests upon a firmer foundation than the latest happy event. Fundamentally, it is based on the one-time, every way unique event that took place on the cross. It derives its lasting quality from the fact that the cross was but the beginning of that event; not the end. There was also an empty tomb and an ascension to the throne of God. That multifaceted event is the event of all events. It is the event that, properly understood, colors all other events, making them a blessing

---

1 The Hebrew word used in this Psalm is *ashre*. According to *The Dictionary of Old Testament Theology and Exegesis*, the term "blessed" means "to be called fortunate," "to be called happy" (Vol. I, p. 568).

to those who possess that understanding. And it alone has the staying power to bring about lasting happinesses.

How that happens is the concern of this book. How you may become a participant in these happiness reverberations, which like an infinite circle of concentric ripples extends to all eternity, is another. The first Psalm speaks of multiple happinesses because the writer wanted to explain the lasting quality of what he was talking about. A quality that the world seeks, but looks for in all the wrong places, in all the wrong ways.

Christians, who fail to enter into the joys of the Easter event, and who lead sad, miserable lives when they can lead supremely happy ones, need to hear what the Psalmist says. His message is not for the unbelieving sinner alone. Indeed, it seems to be primarily aimed at the believer. Either way, there is much for you – whether or not you are a Christian – in Psalm 1. Listen, and learn!

Chapter Two
IT'S GOD FROM WHOM ALL BLESSINGS FLOW

"Blessings," we have seen, are those favors shown to His children by God in Whom they originate. As we shall see in this Psalm, while they originate in and flow from Him, ordinarily, blessings also involve attitudes and actions on the part of the believer as well. In other words, the human and the divine work together.

When I say that, I certainly do not mean to imply that they work on an equal basis. Everything that brings about happiness in the life of a Christian, including his willingness to obey and his ability to do so,[1] stems from God. So that human agency in the process is itself a part of the divine means of bringing about blessing. Therefore, we can rightly sing (as we

---

1 Cf. Philippians 2:13.

do in the doxology), "Praise God from Whom all blessings flow."

Blessing, or divinely-given happiness, may persist not only as a steady, ongoing element of life, coloring all that one does, but unlike humanly-devised "happiness," it persists even in the midst of sorrow, hardship, persecution and trials of every sort. Since it does not depend upon happenings, as we have seen, but upon the favor of God, it transcends events here on earth. The heavenly dimension so colors those events that they are seen not only in terms of their effect upon one's temporal, personal affairs but also as representing God's goodness to believers – even when that is difficult to discern at the moment.

Several years ago, I started to write a book. Here's how it began:

> I am high up in the mountains of Sequoia National Forest at Hume Lake Bible Conference grounds. There is snow on the mountain peaks and some along the roadside. The air is crisp, trout fishing is more than adequate, and the food is excellent. All-in-all

it would seem that this is the perfect setting for a book about how God blesses his servants.

But I was all off base in writing such words. Certainly, now and then, God grants us such idyllic times as these, but more often than not His blessings come in the midst of the grime and crime of the city, in the trials and heartaches of ministry, in the troubles and pain of old age and in the battles for truth and righteousness (within and without) that more frequently characterize our lives.

The problem is that so often, we fail to discern those blessings and, therefore, fail to enjoy them. Like Peter walking on the waves, we look at the water splashing around us instead of keeping our eyes fixed on the Lord – and we begin to sink. It is time for those "untold blessings" that – like the dew – are new every morning, to be told!

The Psalm is designed to map out the road to happiness; it points the way to the way. Many who have set out to glorify God, fail to "enjoy Him forever."[2] They have become bogged down in the daily grind of routine activities that life

---

2 At least during the earthly part of the journey.

requires. Initial glimpses of the glory of work done for Christ have faded. Some are ready to throw in the towel because, as they would put it, they have "beat their heads against the wall once too often." All such sentiments come from a failure to enjoy the happiness that believers may have as it is set forth in Psalm one.

Unlike many books written by Christians today, I am not interested in filling pages with personal stories and testimonies. Why? Because no lasting joy or comfort may be derived from such sources. If you thought there was, in time you probably would end up saying, "Yeah, that's just fine for them, but I'm not they, and my situation is not theirs. And, what's more – how is it that they seem to get all the breaks and I don't?" No, the only route to happiness is found in God's Word, the Scriptures of the Old and New Testaments. And, because those inspired writings were recorded for every child of God, the encouragements found therein pertain to every faithful believer, regardless of his circumstances. The encouragements to enjoy blessednesses from God rest not on the uncertain testimonies of men, but on the unfailing promises of God. Any examples that you encounter in this book, therefore, are offered only to help explicate or direct you to biblical principles; they are not the foundation for blessing itself.[3]

In conjunction with what I have just noted, you will notice where the Psalmist says one's "delight" is found: in God's "law." As we shall see, the law of God means His divine revelation of Himself and His will for man. In other words, the delight – which is no mean element in all true blessing – is in God Himself and in the disclosure of His purposes for His own. It is the pleasure of knowing that one is on the right road – the one that, in the "company of the righteous," leads to God himself.

So, having treated such initial concerns, let us dig into the Psalm to see more about what God has to say about the road to happiness.

---

[3] Christian teaching must never be drawn from experience; experience must be understood in terms of biblical teaching. But, having done so, it is often helpful to illustrate how that teaching applies to, and is actually fulfilled in, life today. The authority must always come from Scriptural truth; never from our experience of it.

Chapter Three
WALK, STAND, SIT

Probably, you have noticed that there are three verbs prominently mentioned in verse 1: walked, stood, sat. These verbs have to do with what the blessed, or happy, person does not do. Let's look carefully at them. They are set forth in conjunction with the three words wicked, sinners, and scoffers. What is it that the writer of the Psalm is telling us by connecting these six words? Several things.

First, he is making it clear that there are many who are heading toward destruction because they have taken the wrong road. It is a road that leads away from God and His will. He refers to this wrong route as the "counsel," the "way" and the "seat," three words, again, connected with the other six, making nine matched words in all. These nine words are arranged in sets of three each, as follows:

walked … counsel … wicked

stood … way … sinners

sat … seat … scoffers

In addition, this succession of three threes, that I have set out plainly before you, clearly show how sin processes. It is an admirable description of how one slowly, by increments, becomes so entirely opposed to the things of God that he may end up scoffing at them.

The writer not only wants to warn the unbeliever, to turn him from the error of his way, but likewise, he wants the worldly believer as well to take heed. The Psalmist wants all true followers of the Lord to know and enjoy the happy life. When they follow unbelieving ways and adopt worldly thoughts and habits, they miss out on many of the joys expressed in this Psalm. How do believers get entangled in worldly ways?

The incremental process begins with pitching one's tent toward Sodom, as Lot did (Genesis 13:12, 13). Lot, a believer, failed to reckon with the fact mentioned in verse 13 – the men of Sodom were "extremely wicked sinners against the Lord." With thought only of the luxury and ease afforded by the verdant valley of the Jordan, he exposed himself and his family to the influence of this wretched environment. Ultimately, he ended up among the elders of the city![1]

Similarly, people today move from one location to another for some temporal advantage, such as obtaining a more lucrative job, giving little thought to what sort of churches may or may not be located nearby. They leave God out of the decision. Too late, they discover that it is no place for raising a family. There is no vital congregation in which they or their children may grow while feeding upon regular, faithful preaching of the Word and the fellowship of God's people. In time, they may become mere hangers on to some nominal Christian church, or drift completely away from church altogether. In both places, they will be fed more and more of the counsel of the wicked.

The Psalmist puts it more generally. The first exposure to a destructive lifestyle of

---

[1] See Genesis 19:8: "sitting in the gate" meant sitting in the gate house (or city hall) as an elder.

misery (rather than happiness) is to "walk in the counsel of the wicked." To begin with, the believer has no idea of joining them or – heaven forbid! – becoming a leading scorner among them. No, he begins his downward descent by simply listening to the "counsel" of the wicked, and walking accordingly.

To "walk" is a biblical expression that means to live day by day in a certain way. To speak of the Christian's *walk*, is to designate what, over a period of time, has become his lifestyle. And it all begins with adopting the *counsel* of the wicked, which advises and directs him in all the wrong things.

This counsel is the philosophy, the ideas, and the attitudes of those who do not know God. It has to do with what it is that builds one's *weltenshauing*, or world-view. The key element in a worldly world-view is the attempt to become autonomous; to divorce God from one's life, stressing one's independence of Him. This was the devil's ploy in the Garden of Eden. In effect, he told Eve that God forbade the fruit because He was afraid that she and her husband would become independent of Him. If they ate, they would become like God. They would no longer need to submit to and learn from Him. This godless *counsel* is still at the nerve center of all that is taught in the devil's school today. His line has not changed in that regard.

Too many Christians are worldly. That means, preeminently, that they think, believe, and act as the world does. They are caught up in their culture. What God told the people through Isaiah is apropos: "Your ways are not My ways, and your thoughts are not My thoughts" (Isaiah 55:8). That is the essence of the problem; the "counsel" of the ungodly leaves God out of the picture while attempting to live life autonomously. The wicked do not consider whether or not there is a good, Bible-believing church in the community into which they may move. Their consideration is but for the temporal advantages they can receive.

Many Christians, though they would deny it in horror, live as if God means nothing more to them than going to church a couple of hours on Sunday. For all practical purposes, they have all but divorced Him from the rest of life. Consequently, they live a life not too different from the life of the unbeliever. That is because they follow the counsel – i.e., the advice, directions, principles, practices, and the example – of the world. "Oh, why are you so narrow?" they may ask other, more serious Christians. "Why do you spend so much time doing things at church? You should be involved in politics more, you could spend more time watching sports events, you don't really know enough of what goes on in the world to be able to talk about, let alone live, in it!" That is the sort of attitude that is soon developed by those who "walk" (begin to live their lives according to) the counsel of the wicked.

"But, I abhor wickedness; I don't walk in the ways of the wicked," someone may protest. Don't be too sure. This word "wicked" does not refer necessarily to *notorious* sinners, as does the word "sinners" in the second set of three words we shall look at presently. Rather, those of whom it speaks are the garden variety, run of the mill unbelievers, who without much thought simply follow their own sinful propensities to live lives apart from God. All sin – particularly the attempt to ignore God – is wickedness. If you were to ask compromising Christians about their "counsel," most of them would be hard-pressed to sum up the wicked philosophy of life. They have imbibed the philosophic counsel of the wicked slowly, imperceptibly. As you speak to them, it isn't long before you detect them mimicking those around them. You hear them saying such things as "Live and let live," "What goes around, comes around," "You only go round once," and the like. This unconsciously-derived counsel amounts to saying, "Don't do anything that might lead to your unhappiness," when unwittingly the outcome of all they do produces, at best, the sort of human temporal "happiness" described above. True happiness, available to all Christians who have not walked in the counsel of the wicked, eludes them. But it is time to consider the second word in the second series – "walk."

Chapter Four
STANDING ... THEN SITTING

Yes, it all begins with the "counsel of the ungodly (wicked)" persons. When a believer begins to take heed to the philosophy, the advice, and the wisdom of the world, he has embarked on the way of misery rather than the road to happiness. He does not know this, and for a time thinks just the opposite about his decision to do so.

As a result of this wayward course he soon finds himself *standing* in the *way* (path) of *sinners*, which is the second stage mentioned by the Psalmist as he describes a person's descent into the depths of unrighteousness. At first, like Lot, he merely pitched his tent *toward* Sodom by listening to and beginning to heed wicked counsel. At that point, he is said to be "walking" in this counsel. That is to say, he pays enough attention to it that he buys into it so as to end up following it. At first, this ungodly counsel seems strange, perhaps even contradictory to what he reads in Scripture. But the longer he listens to it, and the less he reads his Bible (and frequents the preaching of the Word), the more it seems to make sense. Eclectically oriented, he is now able to find ways of justifying very unbiblical ideas. He may hear and accept the misleading slogan "All truth is God's truth." No one mentions the corollary: "All error is the Devil's error." Therefore, he fails to recognize that there must be a standard to discern between the two (the Bible). Soon, he develops friendships with other worldly Christians and unbelievers who reinforce his errant beliefs by *their* counsel. And so it goes, until sooner or later he is on the same road as hardened "sinners."

Hengstenberg says that the word *hata* ("sinners") in this verse refers to the wicked with respect to their "lengthened series of sinful acts." What he means by this is that these people are habitual sinners. They sin in some way not only once or twice, but have adopted patterns of sin that constitute their belief systems and lifestyles. While each person's sinful patterns may constitute his own peculiar style of sinning, it has become just that – a lifestyle, or (in biblical terms) a "walk."

Lot, who pitched his tent toward Sodom is, as we next find him, living *in* Sodom. He has become accustomed to the ways of the Sodomites. He has become caught up in their counsel and their way of life.

What a warning there is in this for Christians! I have known pastors who have believed in the truths of God's Word and preached them faithfully – for a time. But, somewhere along the way, they became intrigued with the views of pagan psychologists and psychiatrists and left the pastorate. Why? They took training under unbelieving professors, adopted much of their counsel, and soon were so enamored with it that they ended up leaving the ministry to become psychologists or psychiatrists themselves. Early on, they reasoned that they were going to become "Christian counselors" by doing so, but it was not long before the counsel they had received overran their Christian beliefs. More than one of them found himself, as a result, trying less and less to integrate Christianity into what he was doing; it was too difficult, unprofitable and (after all) couldn't that be left for the preachers to do?

They had abandoned the way of God for the way of sinners. Soon, they were no different in their counseling beliefs and practices than those whose counsel they imbibed in graduate schools.

In time – usually, not too long after – they found themselves sitting in the seat of the scornful. In contact with those pastors and laymen who remained faithful to the Bible, they soon scoffed at this determination as "foolish, unscholarly, simplistic." From their Christian college or seminary posts, they not only taught these ideas to a generation of students whose parents had paid good money to have them solidified in their faith. Those who refused to go their way were not worth listening to. Such naive persons, as they would often *scornfully* describe them, probably would do more harm than good by their insistence on the sufficiency of the Scriptures.

And, if a student happened to differ (and sometimes merely question) these things, some *avant-garde* professors would lower their grades, and sometimes make such students objects of ridicule and derision. They would be particularly hard on students who might mention biblical counseling or the books and ideas of men in the Nouthetic counseling movement. There still are many "seats of the scornful" in "Christian" higher educational circles today. And they are easily filled!

So, the warning exists: there is a progression into evil that begins with heeding the counsel of the wicked, next moves to becoming involved in their sinful teachings and activities, and finally ends up with scoffing at truth. Every Christian is susceptible to such influences (cf. I Corinthians 15:33). So, "let him who thinks that he stands [in biblical teaching], take heed lest he fall [into error]."

Chapter Five
STAYING OFF THE WRONG ROAD

As Peter pointed out in discussing the sorry plight of Lot – the believer who compromised with sin – in time, he became "sick and tired of the immoral behavior of lawless men" (II Peter 2:7), and he "tortured his righteous soul"[1] (v. 8). The picture is of one who, rather than happy, had become utterly miserable. God will not allow His erring children to go astray without chastising them.

Here, in the Psalm, it is absolutely plain that the brother or sister who chooses the counsel, way, and seat of the wicked has missed the road

---

[1] In mentioning Lot's sin and its consequences, Peter again and again has to identify him as a believer, using the word righteous (i.e., one declared so). Just reading the account of his actions one might not think he was a believer. Notice, he "vexed" or "tortured" himself by living among them!

to happiness. Notice the negative: happinesses come to those who *do not* walk in the counsel, stand in the way, or sit in the seat of the unbeliever. This negative says it all. Happiness comes by following other counsel, standing in a different way, and sitting in quite a different seat. The person who chooses God's way is the one who comes to know true happiness – the lasting happiness of God. Indeed, this felicity is not merely lasting—it is everlasting!

While in what follows, the writer of the Psalm will describe the means of obtaining this happiness, it is interesting to note that he begins by warning the reader that happiness is found in some other lifestyle than the lifestyle of the wicked. That negative emphasis, which is so often decried in our day, the emphasis upon that which is wrong, that is so foreign to relativistic pluralism, is scarcely heard even in churches. In order to be politically correct – or at least "kind and genteel," we are told to accentuate the positive and leave the negative alone. But the writers of Scripture are more realistic. They know that there is a wrong way as well as a right one. Indeed, they recognize that choosing one way is tantamount to rejecting all others. They go even farther: all other ways are stacked up together over against God's way as wrong.

Moreover, the writers of the Scriptures, true to the loving-kindness of God, warn their readers that to take the wrong way is to court disaster. They want their readers to follow the road to true happiness and not to become bogged down on a road that can only lead to misery. Lot found at the end of his progression into sin that he had opted for misery for himself, that he lost his prestige as an elder of the city, that his sons-in-law were destroyed, and that his wife, who had become so enamored with the world of the cities of the plain, was turned into salt. What loss! What misery. And it all could have been avoided if he had carefully weighed the influence of a sinful culture. The trifling advantage of the well-watered plains could hardly be compared with the misery that he knew as a consequence of his poor choice. "O the blessednesses of the man who does not …" That is the important warning to post before the eyes of all, but especially before those who are likely to settle for the easy way, thinking that they are strong enough to combat the evil influences that seem ever to surround such ways. God is concerned to warn as well as to encourage; that is why He begins with the negative: Happiness comes from *not* engaging in some activities.

When issuing warnings, many Christians today will accuse those who do of being legalistic, of being occupied with dos and don'ts. They bring opprobrium upon their heads as if they were interested only in causing their fellow-Christians to walk in stern paths of joylessness. The opposite is true, as this Psalm gives evidence. Don't fall for the "sophisticated" Christian who thinks that he can linger among unbelievers as friend and recipient of worldly wisdom with no adverse effects. Take heed, rather, to I Corinthians 15:33: "Don't be misled. Bad companions corrupt good habits." Notice, the verse says that even when one has acquired good life patterns, they may be torn down by following the ways of bad companions. And – of great interest – Paul knew that people could readily misjudge the matter and be "misled." So, he issued this warning – out of love.

Chapter Six
DELIGHTING IN SCRIPTURE

In contrast to walking in the counsel of the ungodly wicked, the happy believer delights in the law of God. Because this is so, he meditates in it day and night. Now that is certainly an important contrast if there ever was one: walking in wicked counsel versus delighting in God's Word. Few things could be more directly opposed to one another. Here the antithesis that runs throughout the Psalms strongly appears.

When you read the Psalms, you soon discover that the Word of the living God plays a prominent part in what the Psalmists say and do. Indeed, there is one entire Psalm devoted to the law (Psalm 119). That Psalm is a diary of what the Psalmist thought about God's Word as he expressed it in prayer and in instructing others. Expressions of joy, happiness, excitement, confidence, victory characterize that Psalm. It is from God's law that he derives the counsel he needs to live a life pleasing to God and joyous to himself. If you want to know what "delighting" in God's law is all about in life contexts, simply reread Psalm 119!

The word delight, used in Psalm 1, has the idea of being inclined toward something, bending toward it because of the pleasure and delight that it gives. How suggestive that word picture is: rather than finding the way of the world enticing, the Psalmist is attracted, drawn to, God's law. Here is what interests him; not everything else that others find appealing. Are you attracted to God's Word because of the pleasure you receive from reading and following it? If you are not drawn to God's Word over and over again as something that you delight in studying so as to know God's will, surely there is something wrong in your life. You should examine yourself so as to discover what it is and, then, remedy the situation.

A person may not be attracted to the Bible for many reasons. Perhaps he has never learned how to study it. He needs help in doing so.[1] It is possible that he finds the King James English in his Bible forbidding, not realizing that there are translations in modern English. Then, he should get a good modern translation.[2] As a child, he may have had to endure poor preaching that turned him off and, as a result, prejudiced him negatively toward the Bible as a boring book. If so, he should search out a church where the preaching of the Bible is powerful and practical. It is conceivable that he has been misinstructed about the Bible; having been taught that it is full of errors, no wonder he is repelled by Scripture. In that case, he must seek another church, one in which the Bible is respected as the inerrant Word of the living God. We could go on mentioning possible reasons why a Christian fails to appreciate the Bible, why he does not "bend" toward it or delight in it.

Then, too, he may be following the counsel of the wicked. Since the two sources of information are diametrically opposed to one

---

1 For help, see my book *What to Do On Thursday*.
2 Such as the *New American Standard Version*, the *English Standard Version*, or the *Christian Counselor's New Testament and Proverbs*.

another, a person is not likely to be caught up in one of them without rejecting the other as uninteresting, to say the least. The antithesis between the counsel in God's law and man's counsel is such that a thinking person may not hold to both.

At any rate, whatever the reason why a Christian does not find delight in the law of God, he must uncover it and quickly remedy the situation. If he is unable to discover and solve the problem himself, he ought to find a good Bible-believing pastor who counsels Scripturally for help. Otherwise, he is likely not only to miss much joy and happiness; he is likely to end up like Lot!

Because, ultimately, the solution to the problem is to begin to "meditate in the law day and night," it is important to understand what that means. Indeed, until he learns how and does so, he may have an interest in God's law, but he will hardly *delight* in it. Since regular meditation is so important, it will be necessary to devote the next chapter to the matter.

Chapter Seven

MEDITATING IN THE BIBLE

When one "meditates in" the Word of God, it is not the same thing as using many of the modern meditating methods that originated in Eastern cultures. The latter, in essence, takes place when one meditates on his own thoughts. Instead of looking outside of himself for instruction, the oriental meditator "peals the onion," discovering what he himself is thinking about a matter. He is inwardly focused, whereas the Bible mediator focuses outwardly upon revelation that is external to himself. Instead of perusing his own thoughts and trusting his own inner resources, he recognizes his utter dependence upon Another and upon His thoughts. And he calls upon His resources, rather than depending upon his own. The Eastern meditator violates the command of Proverbs 3:5[b], and the biblical meditator follows Proverbs 3:5[a].

What does the word "meditate" mean? The Hebrew *hanah* means to "mutter." It describes someone who is talking to himself. He is discussing the truths of God's law with himself.[1] Why? For several reasons, among which are the following, listed in the sequence in which they may develop during a period of meditation.

First, the Christian meditator talks to himself about the meaning of the Scriptures upon which he is meditating. He asks, "Precisely what do they mean?"[2] He meditates upon the Bible in order to bring divine truth into his thinking. He then asks, "Are the Scriptures which I am considering related to the matter with which I am presently concerned? If so how?" Then, he talks to himself about the

---

[1] Plainly, the Christian meditates within himself (cf. Psalm 19:15). But the materials used in the process to define and solve problems are from without.

[2] When he cannot answer this question with precision he must stop meditating and spend time studying the passage until he thoroughly understands what God was saying in it. The sort of meditation in which "devotions" mean using a passage without understanding to stir the emotions is a wrong-headed use of meditation and a travesty upon the Scriptures.

matter itself: "Hmmm? Exactly what is it that I am confronting, and what do I need to know from God's Word about it?" He then brings the issue and the Scriptures together into a fruitful conjunction so that he may determine God's view of the matter. Having understood this, he goes on to discuss (with himself) biblically-oriented ways and means of reaching a solution to the problems that are involved. And, finally, he plans when and how he must go about putting the plan into action. One fruitful way to meditate is to do so with pencil and paper in hand to jot down conclusions.

True meditation, then, always issues in some *biblical* change in the thinking of the person meditating that ought to lead to a change in his situation that is pleasing to God. Often it will also lead to a change in his actions and his lifestyle. Of course, when a Christian mediates in a biblical fashion, part of that meditation will also include asking God to help him to understand, think, and do all that the Scriptures teach. It may, at times, lead to confession of sin. At each stage he will call upon God for help.

Meditating in the Bible

The believer will not view meditation as a mere technique in which he views the process itself doing something for him; he will see it as a biblical problem-solving method in which the truth of the Bible is comprehended, digested and put to work. Clearly, there is nothing mystical about it. At every point the mind is engaged. It is true that disciplined, regular use of the process ought to change the way in which one thinks and acts, but that is a by-product, not the end or goal of meditation. It is not to be thought of as an experience to be entered into for its own sake, but at a process leading to a result. In effect, meditation on the Word of God means serious thought about issues that produces results that honor and please God.

Now, closely connected to what I have been saying is the word "law." This word, like others that are used to designate the Scriptures, has its own particular nuance.[3] The word law means "to thrust out the finger." The idea behind the figure of speech inherent in the term is that the forefinger points the way. The finger is thrust out to *direct* someone. It is like what the farmer

---

[3] For other words used to describe the Bible see my book, *Counsel from Psalm 119*.

does when he motions and says, "He went that-a-way."

Since the writer described the Bible by this word which emphasizes its directive nature and purpose, it is clear that the one meditating *leans upon Scripture for direction.* This he does rather than depending upon his own understanding. It is also clear that the mystical element that characterizes some meditation is foreign to the entire process which from start to finish is informed and controlled by revelatory information which requires interpretation, application and implementation. Nothing could be farther from Eastern methods.

Notice, also, that this muttering process is carried on "day and night." What does that phrase indicate? It indicates that meditation may take place *at any time.* It is not necessary to set aside a particular time of the day for it. Rather, it seems, whenever it is appropriate, one should meditate. Usually, some event that occurs, some decision to be made, some problem to be solved – or the like – will *trigger* a time of meditation. Instead of turning elsewhere for help, occasions like these ought to bring on a time of meditation. It is not inappropriate to meditate when mowing the lawn, when taking a walk or when sitting at a desk *so long as the Bible passages used are available and properly understood.* This latter qualification is in the text – one meditates *in the law of the Lord.* There is no such thing as Christian meditation apart from the Bible.

Obviously, one may "hide God's Word in his heart" (Psalm 119:11) so that it is available to him as he goes about his business during the day (or night). But it is also true that if he does not know what Scripture says about a matter of concern, he had better take the time and make the effort to search the Scriptures and study them. Otherwise, one may deceive himself into thinking that he is meditating biblically when he is not. Mediataion runs out of steam when the fuel of the Bible runs low.

"Day and night" also has in it the idea of regularity. One does it *throughout* the day. He does not limit himself to one part of the day or one time. Neither does he restrict his meditation to just some kinds of matters. *Whatever* arises as a question, at any time of the day, may deserve meditation upon. There is no matter too large or too small. This process, by which one brings the Bible to bear upon all of the issues of life, is one that ought to be employed frequently. Thus, daily meditation is a way of becoming more and more saturated with the Word of God. It is a way of growing more and more like Christ. It is a way of listening to His counsel rather than to the counsel of the wicked. Throughout life's various events, one meditates upon God's law in order to find His "way." By doing so, he soon finds himself on the road to happiness toward which God's *torah* (law) points him.

Chapter Eight
LIKE A TREE

If the person who delights in the *torah* (law) meditates in it day and night in order to find the direction it points in various life situations, what sort of blessings may he expect to follow? That is what verse 3 is all about. In that verse the writer sets forth in a figurative description of what the "happy" way is like:

Now, he will be like a tree that is planted by irrigating canals

    Which will give forth its fruit in its season.

    And its leaf will not wither.

    And everything that he does he will cause to prosper.

Three things are noted in that description: a constant source of water, verdant leaves and the proper sort of fruitfulness. Let's examine each.

The source of water that the tree has is provided by man-made canals. The importance of this is that there is no lack. The dry gulch (or "wadi") of Palestine is famous for the fact that it was not a dependable water source. The canal, on the other hand, was designed so that even in dryer times water would still be provided.

That picture is provocative. The believer will go through his dry periods. Money may be scarce, sickness may overtake him, difficulties in a world set against the truth of God may arise, and so on. But, if he is following the way pointed out by the *torah*, he will always have sustenance. This is precisely what the apostle Paul told us when he wrote "We are afflicted in all sorts of ways,[1] but not crushed; perplexed, but not given to despair; persecuted, but not deserted; struck down, but not destroyed" (II Corinthians 4:8, 9). Hard times may come, but the water source is unfailing: "As a result, we don't give up, even though our outer person is decaying, because out inner person is being

---

[1] For lists of these trials see II Corinthians 6:4–10; 11:23–29).

renewed daily" (II Corinthians 4:17). Plainly, this is what the Psalmist had in mind when he penned this description of the tree "planted by [literally, 'over'] the watering canals." The picture is of a tree that is planted so close to the water in a canal that its branches hang "over" it.

The words of Paul, however, make it clear that there is strength, refreshment and sustenance *within*. What one sees on the outside may not approximate what is within. Thus, the condition of the body, and other outward circumstances, may deceive. One's physical state may be going to wrack and ruin but, inwardly, he may still be growing stronger and stronger by the grace God gives to sustain him in the face of old age, hardship and trial. Christians need not "give up" when hard times come; they are planted by the watering canals. There is no end to the amount of encouragement, assurance and inner stability that God can give. Indeed, there is nothing that comes into a believer's life that he cannot handle if he handles it God's way (I Corinthians 10:13). He never has to "give up" because he has run out of grace. The grace of God is boundless.

The second aspect of the figure that is mentioned is the unwithering leaves of the tree. Because it is served by canals, there is no time when it need dry up because of a lack of water. The concept of leaves that do not wither, but remain green even in drought, simply intensifies the idea of continued sustenance. But it also speaks of the *contrast* that exists between such a tree and those that are *not* planted near a source of sustenance. They may wither when there is a lack of water. The picture, therefore, is of one who is "green," when the lives of others are drying up.

The Christian who is on the road to happiness has a testimony to the world. Like the ancient martyrs who faced persecution and death for their Lord, he too stands out among others as verdant in such times. Christians who are not able to bear a witness to others in the dry days of life have ceased to draw upon the source of nourishment that is available to them.

The words of the Psalm ought to be an encouragement to those who must face trials of various sorts; they should reassure believers that God will neither leave nor forsake them, but will use the droughts of their lives as an opportunity for them to testify to His sustaining grace. In the hospital bed, for instance, they may bear a powerful witness to all who come in to visit. And their cooperative spirit and ability to endure pain, may speak loudly to doctors and nurses. If they fail their Lord by becoming brown rather than green at such times, they misrepresent Him. The reason why some Christians wither like the trees around them – those that are not planted by the canals – is because they fail to draw sustenance from God's Word; they do not delight in it and meditate upon it day and night. If your life is drying up, believer, it is time to send your roots deeply into the truths of the Bible!

Lastly, the tree will bear its fruit in season. At the time when it is appropriate for it to do so (in season) the tree will be full of luscious fruit. Whatever works of faith that the believer ought to bear for the honor of God and the blessing of others will be available for those who must pick the fruit. They will not come looking for fruit and find none when it ought to be present. Rather, it will be there precisely when needed (in season). The seasonable appearance of fruit means that at the time when it is expected, it will be available. The Christian is dependable. He will produce; not make promises that he will not keep. Others may count on him to come through even when it is difficult to do so.

The Bible not only *directs* him in his responsibilities but it also *encourages* him to continue faithfully in the performance of them. In it he finds strength to carry on even in the face of opposition and difficulties of various sorts. Once more, the reason for his dependability is found in his meditation in the *torah*. The entire Psalm is extolling God's Word at every point.

The figure of the green tree, sustained by the resources that God provides, is not simply a picture of prosperity (it is that), but also of a life that is fruitful. The concept of prosperity follows in the words, "everything he does, he will cause to prosper," which must be the concern of the next chapter.

Chapter Nine
THE HUMAN AND THE DIVINE

"Isn't it the Holy Spirit Who makes the changes in our lives? Isn't it He Who produces the 'fruit' of the character qualities that are found in Galatians 5? Isn't He the One Who dwells and works within us?"

Yes. Yes. Yes.

"Well, then, how is it that, in speaking of the believer, the Psalmist says that 'Everything that he does he will cause to prosper?' Is it he or the Spirit who does so?"

Here is an interesting fact – as the original indicates – the believer *himself* "causes" prosperity in his own life. That might seem to say that he, instead of the Holy Spirit, does so. But that is not true. And in the understanding of the facts involved lies an important truth.

People are always going wrong by tending too far in one extreme or the other. On the one hand, they incline toward "self-help," by which they ignore or minimize the work of the Spirit. On the other hand, they may so emphasize His place in the life of the believer that the believer himself becomes a passive entity. Both ideas are false, biblically.

The fruit of the Spirit, for instance, is His fruit – certainly. But it is not He Who loves, He Who expresses joy, He Who exhibits patience, and so on. It is the believer. It is *he* who shows love toward God and his neighbor. It is *he* who rejoices in trials as well as in easier times. It is *he* who shows patience when others are frustrated, and during times of pain, sorrow or persecution. How are these things true?

The answer is simple, but profound. And in light of the tendencies to emphasize either the human to the exclusion of the divine, or the divine to the exclusion of the human, the fact is very important. What is it? Simply this: The believer obeys God's command, but he does so by the wisdom and the power of the Spirit. The two work together so that in various places man is said to do something that in other passages is attributed to the Spirit. There is no inconsistency or contradiction here. The Spirit *enables* the Christian to obey.

As he studies the Word of God, the Spirit enlightens him so that he may understand its teachings and discover how they apply to his situation. It is also the Spirit Who encourages and makes the believer willing to do the things that please God (Philippians 2:13). And as he puts his hand to the plow, it is the Spirit Who, by His Word, encourages, strengthens and impels him forward. It is all of the Spirit while, at the same time, it is all of the believer. The two work cooperatively whenever the latter prospers as the Psalm says. It is not against the will or desires of the believer who does the works, but, rather, it is He Who so changes and molds those desires as to make him willing. The idea of the canals of water represent the work of the Spirit that makes it possible for the believer to prosper.

So, self-help is not taught in the Bible. Nor is quietism.[1] Rather, the doctrine of grace is taught. In a believer's life grace takes the form

---

1 The doctrine that God "does it" for and instead of the believer.

of help that enables him to successfully obey God's Word. That is why the Psalmist, who shows great insight into the workings of the human mind, says "everything that he does he will cause to prosper." When a man follows God's Word, delighting in its directions, he will do all those things that will cause him to prosper.

How is that true if he is persecuted, suffers, is poor and the like? What of this promise of prosperity? Many Christians have physical and financial troubles. John, for instance, prayed that Gaius might prosper and be in health – *just as his soul was prospering* (III John 2). The clear inference in those words is that Gaius was inwardly prospering much better than he was outwardly. His physical and financial affairs probably were lagging behind his spiritual affairs.

Well, what of the promise? Physical, material prosperity may not come because the believer fails to delight and meditate in God's Word. And, even when he does, it may all be an intellectual matter – he may fail to put into practice what he reads and understands. That certainly is one possibility.

But what of the Christian who faithfully obeys, yet often finds himself behind the eight ball financially or physically? Surely, the promises of God do not fail in such cases, do they? Of course not. Well, then, how are they fulfilled? Clearly, in such ways as John said they were being fulfilled in the life of Gaius. Here was a man walking in the truth, as John indicates. Yet, he had been thrown out of the church by an unscrupulous pastor named Diotrophes for entertaining missionaries! He disobeyed the jealous requirement that was set down by this self-interested pastor who did not want to share the limelight with the missionaries and was put out of the church. John writes to comment and to encourage him, saying that he had done the right thing. And, in addressing Gaius, he uses a customary salutation about health and success in a unique way by adding his own twist to it: "even as your soul is prospering." One may cause everything he does to prosper as Gaius and Paul by the Spirit, did.

What, then, does it mean to "prosper?" The Hebrew word means "to go through." That, as we say, means to get through something successfully. It pictures one who has a task to perform who, though there may be obstacles to overcome, "makes it" through them all. In short, he succeeds. Now, the prosperity of which the Psalmist speaks is the prosperity that God enables him to bring about in his life by means of the Word and the Spirit. That sort of prosperity may not be material prosperity.

Listen, again, to the Lord Jesus, "Store up treasures in heaven for yourselves, where neither moth nor rust can ruin them, not thieves can dig through and steal." (Matthew 6:20). These "treasures in heaven," which are the result of spiritual prosperity, are far better than material ones, as Jesus pointed out. They cannot be stolen and they do not deteriorate. Moreover, we cannot take the earthly treasures of our material prosperity with us when we die. But the treasures that we send ahead will be waiting for us at death; and they will be eternally ours!

Doubtless, reflecting on Jesus' words, Peter wrote:

> Let us praise the God and Father of our Lord Jesus Christ, Who according to His great mercy regenerated us to a living hope through the resurrection

of the dead, for an incorruptible, unspotted and unfading inheritance that has been kept in the heavens for you who are guarded by God's power through faith for a salvation that is ready to be revealed in the last time (I Peter 1:3–5).

Now, which is greater? Obviously, the heavenly prosperity that awaits us. But the heavenly inheritance may be entered into at least partially in this life. That is to say, the peace and joy that one knows now in the midst of trial and difficulty is itself a foretaste of the perfect *shalom* of the heavenly life.[2] If prosperity does not come your way, Christian, there is nothing but you, yourself, hindering the spiritual success that may rightly be the portion of everyone who avoids the counsel of the wicked, who delights in the law of the Lord, and who meditates upon it day and night.

---

2 *Shalom* means prosperity of the fullest sort. It involves peaceful conditions in which outward prosperity rules.

Chapter Ten
THE WICKED

With one sweep of the brush, the writer of the Psalm negates all that he has said of the righteous: "Not so are the wicked." Because they trust in the counsel of others like themselves the wicked know nothing of the liberating and joyous teachings of God's *torah*. This directive law, unknown to them, does not guide their feet as it does the feet of the godly person (cf. Psalm 27:11; Psalm 119:105). As a result, their feet are often found in slippery spots (Psalm 73:18). Their path is full of difficult and dangerous hills and valleys over which the traveler must find his own way with no trustworthy guide to depend upon. He is on his own in this confusing world of sin! He has nothing more than the counsel of other unsaved persons like himself. He makes decisions, but is never absolutely sure that they are the right ones. He turns to the right and to the left, only to find them false ways that he must re-travel back to the main road again and again. He is "lost," as Jesus put it, with no one to save him from destruction.

There are, of course, happy times buoyed up by the waves of new and exciting things. But, like waves, they have no substance; they do not last. They ever change from day to day, leaving but their flotsam upon the foam spewed upon the shore of his life. The pleasures of sin are short-lived, as we noted earlier in this book. So, the weary traveler, plods his way from birth to death, never knowing why he is here, what he should do and where he is headed. It is a fearful existence; indeed, it can be called little more than that – a mere existence.

He is caught up in trivia. He follows his favorite team, but finds that they let him down as they fail to achieve what he hopes for them. And, when he dares to think about it at all, he recognizes the futility of such activities. Sports, entertainment, politics – they are all but for passing the time. And time, time itself, becomes a dreaded thing as he has it "on his hands" today but fears its shortness tomorrow.

All the dreams he dreamed, drowned in despair, crowd together in enormous bunches of unfulfilled aspirations at the end of life. For what did he live, anyway? How was one to live this miserable existence?

"Not so are the wicked." What a terrible pronouncement. "But do these words apply only to those who are especially evil?" you ask. "After all, not all of my unsaved neighbors are *wicked*, so far as I can see." To think that way is to misunderstand the Psalmist. His word for the unsaved is "wicked." He views all those who do not acknowledge the Lord as their Lord and His Word as their delight as "wicked." After all, what could be more wicked than to go one's own way, sinning in unbelieving lack of repentance and ignoring the revelation given to mankind? What could be more wicked than to substitute the counsel of men for the counsel of God? Preeminently, what could be more wicked than to refuse God's way of salvation through the sacrifice of His Son? No, in his eyes, unbelief is wickedness.

The unsaved have no future: "the lamp of the wicked will be put out" (Proverbs 24:20). His religious expressions are rejected by the Lord: "The sacrifice of the wicked is an abomination. How much more when he brings it with evil intent!" (Proverbs 21:27). And he is always at odds with the righteous: "Those who forsake the law praise the wicked, but those who keep the law strive with them" (Proverbs 28:4). They are always in jeopardy in this life, whether they know so or not, and all their lives they live in "slavery" because of their "fear of death" (Hebrews 2:15). Temporary happiness? Yes. But there is no deep seated certainly, no unshakable peace, no power to overcome temptation, sin and its consequences. The wicked are truly in an unenviable condition. In the middle of the Psalm stands this tragic, but pregnant sentence: "Not so are the wicked." Think of all of the blessings that belong to the believer, both here and throughout eternity. Then, scrawl a huge X over all. That is the condition of the wicked. Not one of the God-given blessings of the righteous is his.

He is in this deplorable state because he has never been regenerated by the Holy Spirit, never trusted Jesus Christ as his Savior, never learned what it means to be transformed into a "new creation." He has never depended upon the death and resurrection of Jesus Christ for the forgiveness of his sins. He is still "in his sins." If you are an unbeliever, you need to trust Christ as your own Lord and Savior if you would not have this terrible description – "not so is the wicked" – chiseled upon your gravestone.

Chapter Eleven
WIND-DRIVEN SOULS

When the Psalmist wrote of the wicked that they are "only like chaff that the wind drives away," he penned a multi-packed thought. There is a possible indication of God's opinion of the wicked in the word "only" (a probable translation overlooked in some versions). He is saying that they are *nothing more than chaff.* The wicked like chaff, among other things, means that they are light (non-substantive) and worthless. Those thoughts are not welcome in many quarters.

Often, Christians themselves, speak of the value of humanity as if all men are of great worth. While I certainly do not intend to get into a long argument here about the matter, I do want to mention the error of that notion. For my fuller biblical argument on the matter, please see my book, *Self-Esteem, Self-Love and*

Self-Image in the Bible. In that volume I have set forth ample reason to refute the teaching. For here, it is necessary, perhaps, only to mention that the Psalmist, speaking for God, views the wicked as "chaff."

Chaff is the light, worthless residue that is blown away by the wind when the grain is tossed into the air. The heavier, substantive material that is used for food drops on the winnowing floor and is by that means separated out from the chaff. When John the Baptist came preaching, he referred to this process by declaring that the Savior had "His shovel in His hand" and that "He will gather His wheat into the barn, but the chaff He will burn with unquenchable fire" (Matthew 4:12). The pile of chaff that remained after the rest of it was blown away, was shoveled up and used for fuel. From the way that John describes Jesus' actions toward the unbelieving chaff, surely *He* could not have had a very high opinion of them. It is time for us to recognize that unbelief is truly wickedness, and that the Lord will dispose of it.

The other aspect of the figure of the chaff is its extreme lightness. It is worthless because it has no substance to it. It is so light that the wind from a fan waved before it can blow it away. This same idea is presented in Psalm 62:9: "Surely men of low degree are vanity, and men of high degree are a lie; in the balances they go up; they are altogether lighter than breath." Think of that! God says that men – of high and of low degree alike – are of no more weight than vanity, than a breath. If you gather them all together, place them on the balance, and weigh them, they are of *negative weight* – the balance rises rather than lowers! That is God's estimate of man – apart from Christ. So, the wicked are worthless; of virtually no significance at all. If they claim a high degree, it turns out to be a *lying* estimate of their worth. It is time that we recognized God's estimate of such persons rather than accept the vain speculations of men in which they seek to exalt man!

The wicked have but a negative value. They are of use in demonstrating God's wrath. They are "vessels of wrath" prepared for that very purpose. If there had been no wicked, God could not have justly demonstrated His nature. He could not have punished unfallen creatures. But, as it is, there are those who reject His Son and upon them He may righteously pour out

His wrath.[1] Similarly, there could have been no opportunity to demonstrate His mercy and grace if there had not been fallen creatures who needed forgiveness.

In all of this, the lightness of the wicked in the eyes of God is apparent. Lightness means dishonor, just as the Hebrew word *kabod* ("weight") is used to describe "glory and reputation." The chaff, dishonorable as they are, are burned in unquenchable fire. That is their end. Reader, if you are not sure of your salvation, gain assurance through faith in Christ before it is too late.

---

[1] For more on this matter, see my book, *The Grand Demonstration* in which I work out the implications of Romans 9:11ff.

Chapter Twelve
THE JUDGMENT

The words "Consequently, the wicked will not stand in the judgment" should be sobering to all who read them. The Psalmist now reaches out beyond this life to eternity. In agreement, the New Testament writer declared that "it is appointed for people to die only once, and after that they face judgment" (Hebrews 9:27). The distinction between the righteous and the wicked is not for this life alone; it persists into eternity. That is a sobering thought because once the judgment takes place, there is no change; there are but two companies following death: "the company of the righteous" and that of the "wicked."

The first thing that is apparent is that the Psalmist considered the destiny of the wicked the result of his wicked unbelief. That is the import of the word "consequently." Because he *does* trust in the "counsel" of the world rather than in the "law" of God, living his life accordingly, he will end up excluded from the "company of the righteous" in the judgment. The two counsels determine the difference.

Have you ever thought about the fact that truth is essential to one's eternal future? Many dismiss the issue of what is true and what is false in a cynical manner: "O well, there are as many ideas about that as there are people." It is that kind of continuum thinking that leads men and women astray. Yet, perhaps, it is the norm for our time. Many reject the very notion of truth versus error, of good versus bad, of right versus wrong. Yet, in the judgment, there will not be as many companies as there are people; there will be only two: that of the righteous, who believed the truth, practiced the good and stood for what is right, and that of the wicked who believed error, practiced the bad and backed that which was wrong. The idea of multiple destinies, based upon an endless variety of opinions, is foreign to the Bible. The antithesis that we see in the Psalm comes into its most vivid form when discussing eternity. There are two, and only two companies in the

The Judgment

judgment: that of the righteous and that of the wicked.

So, it comes down to this: every human being is in one or the other company *now*. That same distinction will continue into eternity.[1] It is not always possible for us to determine in this life which company one belongs to. But the judgment will sort out the wheat from the tares. The word "judgment" carries the connotation of *distinction*. One thing is distinguished from another. Often, the Hebrew word is used to speak of the settling of differences between two persons. In Matthew 25, which is a picture of that final judgment, the "sheep" are distinguished from the "goats." Of course, it is in this life when eternal destinies are determined. *"Today"* is the day of salvation (Hebrews 4:7). *Now* is the time to move from the kingdom of darkness into the kingdom of light by trusting Jesus Christ (Colossians 1:13). After death it will be too late.

The wicked are said to be unable to "stand" in the judgment. That word was used much the

---

[1] Jesus pictured unconverted, wicked persons as "judged already" (John 3:18) because of their unbelief. At His first coming He came into the world to save; at the second, He will conduct the final judgment.

way our word is. We say "He hasn't a leg to stand on," when we mean that he hasn't a case that will "stand up" in court. In other words, his mouth will be shut. He will have nothing to say in his defense. The general revelation that God provided in creation should lead the unrighteous to conclude that there is a powerful God, whom they should seek with all their hearts. But, instead, they "suppress the truth" by their unrighteousness (Romans 1:18). "So," concludes Paul, "they are without excuse" (Romans 1:20). To not "stand in the judgment" and to be "without excuse" are two different ways of saying the same thing,

What a fearful thing it is to face the Lord in judgment without a case (Hebrews 10:31)! Referring to Isaiah 26:11, the writer of Hebrews calls the judgment to be meted out "the fury of fire that is going to consume God's adversaries" (Hebrews 1);27). No wonder the Psalmist is concerned to warn his reader of the judgment to come in this Psalm which is the gateway to the rest.

Chapter Thirteen
THE TWO ROADS

We have seen that there are two distinct destinies, one or the other allotted to each human being. These are reached by two distinct roads: the "way of the righteous" and "the way of the wicked" (v. 6). The former, the Psalmist says, "Yahweh knows" but the latter is said to "end in ruin." While the ideas are clear, the exact wording needs a bit of explanation.

"What does it mean when one says that 'Yahweh knows' something? Doesn't He know everything?" Yes, of course. But to "know" may have different meanings in different contexts. Here, the idea of intellectual comprehension is not in view – except very remotely. Rather, the idea is that God knows *with favor*, that He knows *lovingly.* To "know the way of the righteous" is to look favorably upon it. He does so because that "way" (lifestyle) is His way (the one that He has set forth in His law, and of which He approves).

The "way" of the wicked was a lifestyle that can only be condemned for all eternity. Not only did it consist of continual sin and unbelief, but it was one in which the covenant sign and promises were rejected by those who pursued it: "Every person did that which was right in his own eyes" (Judges 17:6). Just as this occurred when "there was no king in Israel" so, too, people today act as if there is no King in heaven.

I mention the breaking of God's covenant promises by Israelites, for whom this Psalm was originally written, because the Psalmist uses Yahweh, the covenant Name of God. He thereby was calling attention to the fact that the reader is sealed to God by covenant. And when he becomes a covenant-breaker, this is utter wickedness. How is that? By covenant, God promised wonderful things to His people which can be summed up in the often-occurring covenant slogan "I will be your God and you will by My people." God elected His people to a special place of favor and blessing. But to follow the counsel of the wicked rather than the law of God was to repudiate all that God had done and would do for those who love and serve Him. It was tantamount to breaking the covenant. God, therefore, would not be the God of those who break His covenant – not now or for eternity. To break the covenant is to take a road that ends not in happiness, but in utter ruin.

The Abrahamic covenant remains today. As was true in Old Testament times, so too today, one keeps the covenant by faith. Today, all who believe in Jesus Christ belong to Yahweh as members of His covenant people. When they are baptized they take upon themselves the current visible sign of membership in the covenant body, the church. Some unbelievers, today, as was true throughout Old Testament history, are a part of the visible body of those who meet in God's Name, purporting to be His people. Yet, their hearts are uncircumcised, they have never been baptized by the Spirit into the inner body of the faithful (I Corinthians 12:13), they lack salvation and they are, therefore, covenant-breakers.

Taking the sign of membership in the visible people of God does not constitute membership in the eternal body of "the righteous." Such persons, like many Israelites, are merely *among* the people, like the "mixed multitude" that came out of Egypt. John speaks to this problem when he mentions some who "went out from us, but they weren't of us; because if they had been of us, they would have remained with us" (I John 2:19). There always have been, and in this life always will be, people who are ingenuine in their profession of faith. Like the wheat that grows together with the tares until the harvest, many of them will not be separated out until the judgment.

The end of the wicked is utter ruin. That is another way of saying eternal punishment in hell, the fury of fire mentioned earlier. Friend, among which company will you stand in the judgment? Do you know? Are you concerned? The only way to be certain of your eternal destiny is to believe in the Lord Jesus Christ – and you will be saved (cf. Acts 16:31). He shed His blood in the place of guilty sinners to bear their punishment for their sin. All those who depend upon Him and what He did will find eternal life in the company of the righteous. All those who do not will not stand in the judgment but will hear those words of utter ruin from the lips of the risen Lord, "Depart from Me, you cursed ones, into eternal fire prepared for the devil and his angels" (Matthew 25:41).

Lightning Source UK Ltd.
Milton Keynes UK
UKHW020716210622
404740UK00012B/1430